W9-DFH-284

Over 12 designs in **Cashsoft**
& **Cashcotton** DK & 4ply
by Martin Storey

Welcome to Classic Holiday, the third brochure in the RYC collection. In it, we feature a collection of DK and 4ply hand knits and crochet designed to be worn for travel and holidays. The accent is on softness and simplicity.

Shot on location in one of the world's most beautiful holiday resorts, this collection is inspired by the serenity and stillness of the nature in high summer. Its tempo is at once thoughtful and nostalgic, reminding us of the past.

Designs include ponchos, wraps and throws that can be slipped on over swimwear or flung over your shoulders in the coolness of evening. Sun tops flatter the face and show off the womanly figure. Charming crocheted bags complete the picture.

To accompany this stunning brochure is a range of wonderfully luxurious yarns in the very best of luxurious natural fibres.

Cashsoft DK and Cashsoft 4 ply comprise a velvety, soft cashmere/wool blend and come in a sumptuous palette of summer colours, including Rose Lake pink, Spa blue, Monet, Weather and Cream.

Cashcotton DK and Cashcotton 4 ply are a blend of cashmere/cotton, offered in a cool summer palette of shades including Chintz and Magenta.

The RYC CLASSIC Collection is a range of hand knits and crochet designed to be a joy to create and a pleasure to wear. Cleverly developed to complement and enrich an existing wardrobe, all the designs will prove much-loved classics.

Martin

Holidays are a time for relaxation, for savouring the simple pleasures
of sunshine, food and wine, being with friends.... Time off asks for soft,
flowing shapes and sleek sun-loving designs.

8 | **Festival** in Cashcotton 4 ply

10 | **Sunskirt** in Cashsoft 4 ply

12 | **Bonbon** in Cashcotton DK

14 | **Sling Bag** in Cashcotton DK

26 | **Beach Coat** in Cashsoft DK

27 | **Swing Bag** in Cashsoft DK

28 | **Candy** in Cashsoft 4 ply

31 | **Travel Bag** in Cashsoft 4 ply

Festival – this softly draping crochet poncho is ideal for travelling. Just fling it over whatever you are wearing....

Crocheted in Cashcotton 4 ply, shown here in Chintz. Pattern instructions page 52

Crocheted in Cashsoft 4 ply, shown here in Rose Lake. Pattern instructions page 58

Sun skirt – a flamenco feel adds a touch of drama to this airy sun skirt, perfect for putting on over your swim wear.

Bonbon – the simplest of vests, this top has fashioned ribbed straps.

Knitted in Cashcotton DK, shown here in Magenta. Pattern instructions page 48

Sling bag – put everything you need for the beach into this capacious crocheted sling bag.

Crocheted in Cashcotton DK, shown here in Magenta. Pattern instructions page 54

Fiesta – light and easy to wear, with its soft fringe, wear this poncho for summer strolls.

Knitted in Cashsoft DK, shown here in Crush. Pattern instructions page 62

Jacuzzi – an airy wrap
is a wonderfully
versatile accessory.
The open-work stitch
used to give a net-like
effect creates the
lightest touch.

Crocheted in Cashcotton DK, shown here in
Apple. Pattern instructions page 53

Sundae – what could be prettier than this feminine camisole with ribbon fastening?

Knitted in Cashsoft 4 ply, shown here in Rose Lake.
Pattern instructions page 60

Carnival – use this crochet shawl, with its swirl design, for summer evenings and siestas in the hammock.

Crocheted in Cashsoft DK, shown here in Tape. Pattern instructions page 63

Both in an airy crochet, this **Beach Coat** and **Swing Bag** make perfect partners. With its flattering long line, the beach coat is ideal to fling over a swim suit or bikini. Fill the bag with your book, sunglasses and something to eat – and head for the sand!

Both designs crocheted in Cashsoft DK and shown here in Sweet. Pattern instructions pages 46 & 55

Candy – a neat, feminine shape is the hallmark of this sleeveless beach top.

Knitted in Cashsoft 4 ply, shown here in Monet. Pattern instructions page 50

Crocheted in Cashsoft 4 ply, shown here in Dive. Pattern instructions page 57

Travel bag – charming yet practical, stow your travel documents in this crochet bag.

Holiday – this delicate wrap encapsulates the beauty of summer on a shimmering day.

Crocheted in Cashsoft 4 ply, shown here in Cream. Pattern instructions page 64

Deckchair – as its name suggests, this shawl takes its inspiration from the seaside. The fringing adds extra softness.

Knitted in Cashsoft DK, shown here in Sweet, Cream & Crush. Pattern instructions page 49

Sorbet – be a bit daring in this ribbed halter-neck sun top. On a hot day, it's all you need.

Knitted in Cashsoft 4 ply, shown here in Spa. Pattern instructions page 56

Knitted in Cashsoft DK, shown here in Glacier. Pattern instructions page 66

Cookie – big beads make a perfect foil for this cross-over halter neck.

Cashsoft DK
Glacier

COOKIE

SLING BAG

BEACH COAT

Cashsoft DK
Sweet

Agapanthus

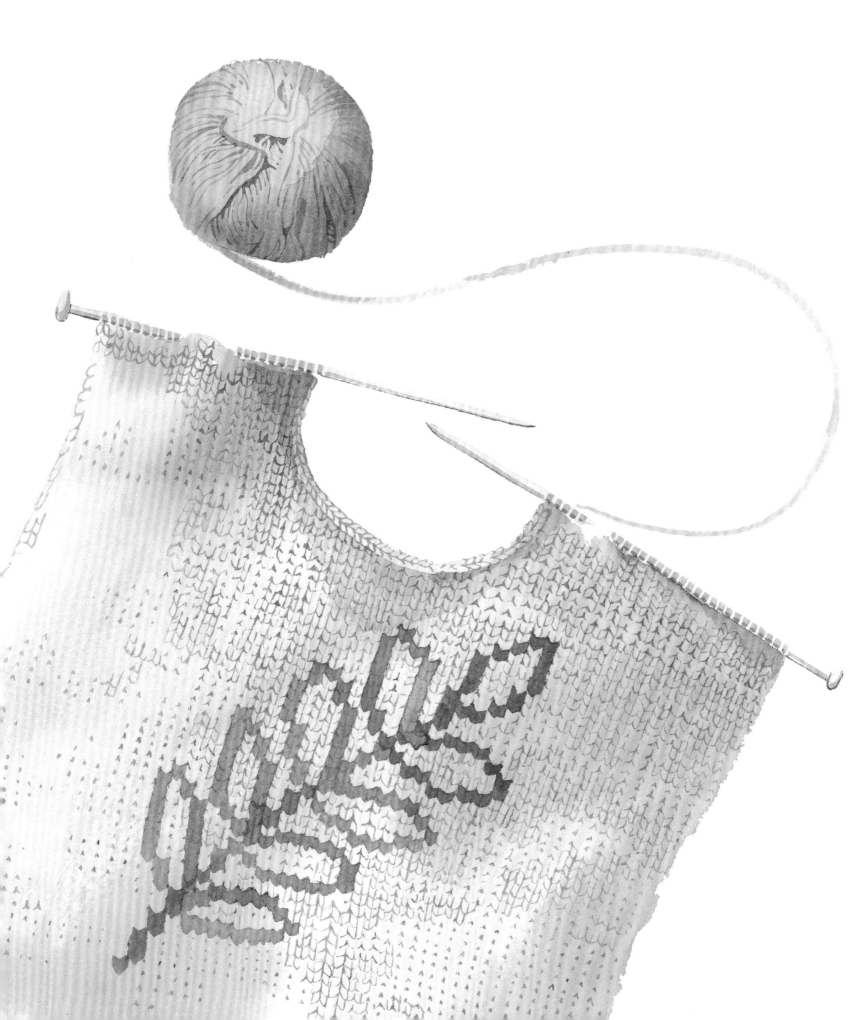

Tension

Obtaining the correct tension is perhaps the single factor which can make the difference between a successful garment and a disastrous one. It controls both the shape and size of an article, so any variation, however slight, can distort the finished garment. Different designers feature in our books and it is **their** tension, given at the **start** of each pattern, which you must match. We recommend that you knit a square in pattern and/or stocking stitch (depending on the pattern instructions) of perhaps 5 - 10 more stitches and 5 - 10 more rows than those given in the tension note. Mark out the central 10cm square with pins. If you have too many stitches to 10cm try again using thicker needles, if you have too few stitches to 10cm try again using finer needles. Once you have achieved the correct tension your garment will be knitted to the measurements indicated in the size diagram shown at the end of the pattern.

Sizing and Size Diagram Note

The instructions are given for the smallest size. Where they vary, work the figures in brackets for the larger sizes. **One set of figures refers to all sizes**. Included with most patterns in this magazine is a **'size diagram'**, or sketch of the finished garment and its dimensions. The size diagram shows the finished width of the garment at the under-arm point, and it is this measurement that the knitter should choose first; a useful tip is to measure one of your own garments which is a comfortable fit. Having chosen a size based on width, look at the corresponding length for that size; if you are not happy with the total length which we recommend, adjust your own garment before beginning your armhole shaping - any adjustment after this point will mean that your sleeve will not fit into your garment easily - don't forget to take your adjustment into account if there is any side seam shaping. Finally, look at the sleeve length; the size diagram shows the finished sleeve measurement, taking into account any top-arm insertion length. Measure your body between the centre of your neck and your wrist, this measurement should correspond to half the garment width plus the sleeve length. Again, your sleeve length may be adjusted, but remember to take into consideration your sleeve increases if you do adjust the length - you must increase more frequently than the pattern states to shorten your sleeve, less frequently to lengthen it.

Chart Note

Many of the patterns in the book are worked from charts. Each square on a chart represents a stitch and each line of squares a row of knitting. Each colour used is given a different letter and these are shown in the **materials** section, or in the **key** alongside the chart of each pattern. When working from the charts, read odd rows (K) from right to left and even rows (P) from left to right, unless otherwise stated.

Finishing Instructions

After working for hours knitting a garment, it seems a great pity that many garments are spoiled because such little care is taken in the pressing and finishing process. Follow the following tips for a truly professional-looking garment.

Pressing

Block out each piece of knitting and following the instructions on the ball band press the garment pieces, omitting the ribs. Tip: Take special care to press the edges, as this will make sewing up both easier and neater. If the ball band indicates that the fabric is not to be pressed, then covering the blocked out fabric with a damp white cotton cloth and leaving it to stand will have the desired effect. Darn in all ends neatly along the selvage edge or a colour join, as appropriate.

Stitching

When stitching the pieces together, remember to match areas of colour and texture very carefully where they meet. Use a seam stitch such as back stitch or mattress stitch for all main knitting seams and join all ribs and neckband with mattress stitch, unless otherwise stated.

Construction

Having completed the pattern instructions, join left shoulder and neckband seams as detailed above. Sew the top of the sleeve to the body of the garment using the method detailed in the pattern, referring to the appropriate guide:

Straight cast-off sleeves: Place centre of cast-off edge of sleeve to shoulder seam. Sew top of sleeve to body, using markers as guidelines where applicable.

Square set-in sleeves: Place centre of cast-off edge of sleeve to shoulder seam. Set sleeve head into armhole, the straight sides at top of sleeve to form a neat right-angle to cast-off sts at armhole on back and front.

Shallow set-in sleeves: Place centre of cast-off edge of sleeve to shoulder seam. Join cast-off sts at beg of armhole shaping to cast-off sts at start of sleeve-head shaping. Sew sleeve head into armhole, easing in shapings.

Set-in sleeves: Place centre of cast-off edge of sleeve to shoulder seam. Set in sleeve, easing sleeve head into armhole.

Join side and sleeve seams.
Slip stitch pocket edgings and linings into place.
Sew on buttons to correspond with buttonholes.

Abbreviations

K	knit
P	purl
st(s)	stitch(es)
inc	increas(e)(ing)
dec	decreas(e)(ing)
st st	stocking stitch (1 row K, 1 row P)
g st	garter stitch (K every row)
beg	begin(ning)
foll	following
rem	remain(ing)
rep	repeat
alt	alternate
cont	continue
patt	pattern
tog	together
mm	millimetres
cm	centimetres
in(s)	inch(es)
RS	right side
WS	wrong side
sl 1	slip one stitch
psso	pass slipped stitch over
tbl	through back of loop
M1	make one stitch by picking up horizontal loop before next stitch and knitting into back of it
yrn	yarn round needle
yfwd	yarn forward
meas	measures
0	no stitches, times or rows
-	no stitches, times or rows for that size

Crochet terms

UK crochet terms and abbreviation have been used throughout. The list below gives the US equivalent where they vary.

Abbrev.	UK	US
dc	double crochet	single crochet
htr	half treble	half double crochet
tr	treble	double crochet

= Easy, straight forward knitting

= Suitable for the average knitter

= For the more experienced knitter

YARN

	XS	S	M	L	XL
To fit bust	81	86	91	97	102 cm
	32	34	36	38	40 in

RYC Cashsoft DK

| | 11 | 12 | 12 | 13 | 14 x 50gm |

(photographed in Sweet 501)

CROCHET HOOKS

3.00mm (no 11) (US D3) crochet hook
3.50mm (no 9) (US E4) crochet hook

BUTTONS – 1 x 75321

TENSION

24 sts and 11 rows to 10 cm measured over pattern using 3.50mm (US E4) crochet hook.

CROCHET ABBREVIATIONS

ch = chain; **dc** = double crochet; **sp(s)** = space(s); **ss** = slip stitch; **tr** = treble; **tr2tog** = yoh and insert hook into next tr, yoh and draw loop through, yoh and draw through 2 loops, miss 1 ch, yoh and insert hook into next tr, yoh and draw loop through, yoh and draw through 2 loops, yoh and draw through all 3 loops on hook; **yoh** = yarn over hook.

BACK

Using 3.50mm (US E4) hook make 116 [122: 128: 134: 140] ch.
Row 1 (RS): 1 tr into 6th ch from hook, *1 ch, miss 1 ch, 1 tr into next ch, rep from * to end, turn.
Row 2: 4 ch (counts as first tr and 1 ch), miss (1 tr and 1 ch) at end of previous row, 1 tr into next tr, *1 ch, miss 1 ch, 1 tr into next tr, rep from * to end, working last tr into 3rd of 4 ch at beg of previous row, turn. 113 [119: 125: 131: 137] sts, 56 [59: 62: 65: 68] ch sps.
Row 2 forms patt.
Cont in patt for a further 48 rows.
Next row: 3 ch (does NOT count as st), miss (1 tr and 1 ch) at end of previous row, 1 tr into next tr – 2 sts decreased, *1 ch, miss 1 ch, 1 tr into next tr, rep from * to last 4 sts, 1 ch, miss 1 ch, tr2tog over next 3 sts – 2 sts decreased, turn.
109 [115: 121: 127: 133] sts.

Working all decreases as set by last row, dec 2 sts at each end of foll 14th row.
105 [111: 117: 123: 129] sts.
Cont straight until back meas 72 [73: 73: 74: 74] cm, ending with RS facing for next row.
Shape armholes
Next row (RS): Ss across and into 5th [7th: 7th: 9th: 9th] st, 3 ch (does NOT count as st), miss 1 ch, 1 tr into next tr, patt to last 7 [9: 9: 11: 11] sts, tr2tog over next 3 sts, turn, leaving rem 4 [6: 6: 8: 8] sts unworked. 93 [95: 101: 103: 109] sts.
Dec 2 sts at each end of next 4 [4: 5: 5: 6] rows.
77 [79: 81: 83: 85] sts.
Work 15 rows. (Armhole should meas 18 [18: 19: 19: 20] cm.)
Shape shoulders and back neck
Next row: Patt 14 [14: 14: 16: 16] sts, tr2tog over next 3 sts and turn, leaving rem sts unworked.
15 [15: 15: 17: 17] sts.
Work each side of neck separately.
Dec 2 sts at neck edge of next row.
13 [13: 13: 15: 15] sts.
Fasten off.
Return to last complete row worked, miss next 43 [45: 47: 45: 47] sts after first shoulder, rejoin yarn to next st, 3 ch (does NOT count as st), miss 1 ch, 1 tr into next tr, patt to end, turn.
15 [15: 15: 17: 17] sts.
Dec 2 sts at neck edge of next row.
13 [13: 13: 15: 15] sts.
Fasten off.

LEFT FRONT

Using 3.50mm (US E4) hook make 60 [62: 66: 68: 72] ch.
Work rows 1 and 2 as given for back.
57 [59: 63: 65: 69] sts, 28 [29: 31: 32: 34] ch sps.
Cont in patt for a further 48 rows.
Working all decreases as set by back, dec 2 sts at beg of next and foll 14th row.
53 [55: 59: 61: 65] sts.
Cont straight until left front matches back to beg of armhole shaping, ending with RS facing for next row.
Shape armhole
Next row (RS): Ss across and into 5th [7th: 7th: 9th: 9th] st, 3 ch (does NOT count as st), miss 1 ch, 1 tr into next tr, patt to end, turn.

47 [47: 51: 51: 55] sts.
Dec 2 sts at armhole edge of next 4 [4: 5: 5: 6] rows.
39 [39: 41: 41: 43] sts.
Work 1 [1: 1: 0: 0] rows.
Shape neck
XS, S and L sizes
Next row (RS): Patt 24 [24: -: 28: -] sts, tr2tog over next 3 sts and turn, leaving rem 12 [12: -: 10: -] sts unworked.
25 [25: -: 29: -] sts.
M and XL sizes
Next row (WS): Ss across and into - [-: 15th: -: 13th] st, 3 ch (does NOT count as st), miss 1 ch, 1 tr into next tr, patt to end, turn. - [-: 25: -: 29] sts.
All sizes
Dec 2 sts at neck edge on next 3 [3: 3: 4: 4] rows, then on foll 3 alt rows. 13 [13: 13: 15: 15] sts.
Work 6 rows.
Fasten off.

RIGHT FRONT

Using 3.50mm (US E4) hook make 60 [62: 66: 68: 72] ch.
Work rows 1 and 2 as given for back.
57 [59: 63: 65: 69] sts, 28 [29: 31: 32: 34] ch sps.
Cont in patt for a further 48 rows.
Working all decreases as set by back, dec 2 sts at end of next and foll 14th row.
53 [55: 59: 61: 65] sts.
Complete to match left front, reversing shapings.

SLEEVES

Using 3.50mm (US E4) hook make 68 [70: 72: 74: 76] ch.
Work rows 1 and 2 as given for back.
65 [67: 69: 71: 73] sts, 32 [33: 34: 35: 36] ch sps.
Cont in patt for a further 1 row.
Next row (WS): 4 ch (counts as 1 tr and 1 ch), 1 tr into tr at end of previous row – 2 sts increased, patt to last st, (1 tr, 1 ch and 1 tr) into 3rd of 4 ch at beg of previous row – 2 sts increased, turn.
Working all increases as set by last row, inc 2 sts at each end of 4th and foll 4th row.
77 [79: 81: 83: 85] sts.
Cont straight until sleeve meas 14 cm, ending with RS facing for next row.

Shape top

Next row (RS): Ss across and into 5th [7th: 7th: 9th: 9th] st, 3 ch (does NOT count as st), miss 1 ch, 1 tr into next tr, patt to last 7 [9: 9: 11: 11] sts, tr2tog over next 3 sts, turn, leaving rem 4 [6: 6: 8: 8] sts unworked. 65 [63: 65: 63: 65] sts. Working all decreases as set by back, dec 2 sts at each end of next and foll 4 alt rows, then on foll 4 rows. 29 [27: 29: 27: 29] sts.
Fasten off.

MAKING UP

Press as described on the information page. Join both shoulder seams using back stitch, or mattress stitch if preferred.
See information page for finishing instructions, setting in sleeves using the set-in method and leaving side seams open for first 39 cm.

Edging

With RS facing and using 3.00mm (US D3) crochet hook, rejoin yarn at base of left front opening edge and work 1 round of dc evenly across left front hem edge, around left side seam opening, across back hem edge, around right side seam opening, across right front hem edge, up right front opening edge, around neck edge and down left front opening edge, working 2 dc into corner points, ensuring edging lays flat and ending with ss to first dc, turn.

Next round: 1 ch (does NOT count as st), 1 dc into each dc to base of right front opening edge, missing dc as required and working 2 dc into corner points to ensure edging lays flat, and making buttonloop at top of right front opening edge by replacing "1 dc into each of next 2 dc" with "3 ch, miss 2 dc".
Fasten off.
Sew on button.

Cuff edging

With RS facing and using 3.00mm (US D3) crochet hook, rejoin yarn at base of sleeve seam and work 1 round of dc evenly around lower edge of sleeve, ending with ss to first dc, turn.

Next round: 1 ch (does NOT count as st), 1 dc into each dc to end, ss to first dc.
Fasten off.

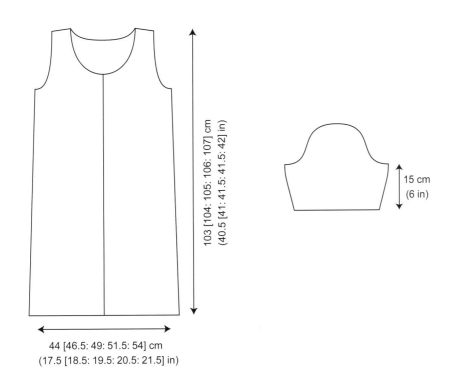

103 [104: 105: 106: 107] cm
(40.5 [41: 41.5: 41.5: 42] in)

44 [46.5: 49: 51.5: 54] cm
(17.5 [18.5: 19.5: 20.5: 21.5] in)

15 cm
(6 in)

Bonbon

YARN

	XS	S	M	L	XL	
To fit bust	81	86	91	97	102	cm
	32	34	36	38	40	in

RYC Cashcotton DK

	3	4	4	4	5	x 50gm

(photographed in Magenta 605)

NEEDLES

1 pair 3¼mm (no 10) (US 3) needles
1 pair 4mm (no 8) (US 6) needles

TENSION

22 sts and 30 rows to 10 cm measured over stocking stitch using 4mm (US 6) needles.

BACK

Using 3¼mm (US 3) needles cast on 85 [91: 97: 103: 109] sts.
Row 1 (RS): K1, *P1, K1, rep from * to end.
Row 2: P1, *K1, P1, rep from * to end.
Rep these 2 rows once more, inc 1 st at end of last row. 86 [92: 98: 104: 110] sts.
Change to 4mm (US 6) needles.
Beg with a K row, work in st st for 8 rows, ending with RS facing for next row.
Next row (RS): K3, K2tog, K to last 5 sts, K2tog tbl, K3.
Work 7 rows.
Rep last 8 rows twice more, then first of these rows (the dec row) again. 78 [84: 90: 96: 102] sts.
Work 9 [11: 11: 11: 11] rows, ending with RS facing for next row.
Next row (RS): K3, M1, K to last 3 sts, M1, K3.
Work 9 rows.
Rep last 10 rows twice more, then first of these rows (the inc row) again. 86 [92: 98: 104: 110] sts.
Cont straight until back meas 31 [32: 32: 33: 33] cm, ending with RS facing for next row.
Shape armholes
Cast off 6 sts at beg of next 2 rows.
74 [80: 86: 92: 98] sts.
S, M, L and XL sizes
Next row (RS): K1, (P1, K1) 5 times, P2tog, K to last 13 sts, P2tog, (K1, P1) 5 times, K1.
Next row: (P1, K1) 6 times, P to last 12 sts, (K1, P1) 6 times.
Rep last 2 rows – [3: 8: 12: 16] times more.

- [72: 68: 66: 64] sts.
All sizes
Next row (RS): K1, (P1, K1) 5 times, P2tog, K to last 13 sts, P2tog, (K1, P1) 5 times, K1.
Next row: (P1, K1) 6 times, P to last 12 sts, (K1, P1) 6 times.
Next row: (K1, P1) 6 times, K to last 12 sts, (P1, K1) 6 times.
Next row: (P1, K1) 6 times, P to last 12 sts, (K1, P1) 6 times.
Rep last 4 rows 11 [9: 7: 5: 4] times more, then first 2 of these rows again. 48 [50: 50: 52: 52] sts.
Shape back neck
Next row (RS): (K1, P1) 6 times, K2 and turn, leaving rem sts on a holder.
Work each side of neck separately.
Next row: P2, (K1, P1) 6 times.
Next row: K1, (P1, K1) 5 times, P2tog, K1.
Work a further 3 rows in rib as set on these 13 sts, ending with RS facing for next row.
Shape shoulder
Cast off in rib.
With RS facing, rejoin yarn to rem sts, cast off centre 20 [22: 22: 24: 24] sts, patt to end.
Complete to match first side, reversing shapings.

FRONT

Work as given for back until 58 [60: 60: 62: 62] sts rem in armhole shaping.

Work 1 row, ending with RS facing for next row.
Shape neck
Next row (RS): Patt 19 sts and turn, leaving rem sts on a holder.
Work each side of neck separately.
Working all armhole decreases as set by back, dec 1 st at armhole edge of 2nd and every foll 4th row until 13 sts rem.
Work 3 rows, ending with RS facing for next row.
Shape shoulder
Cast off in rib.
With RS facing, rejoin yarn to rem sts, cast off centre 20 [22: 22: 24: 24] sts, patt to end.
Complete to match first side, reversing shapings.

MAKING UP

Press as described on the information page.
Join right shoulder seam using back stitch, or mattress stitch if preferred.
Neckband
With RS facing and using 3¼mm (US 3) needles, pick up and knit 24 sts down left side of front neck, 20 [22: 22: 24: 24] sts from front, 24 sts up right side of front neck, 5 sts down right side of back neck, 20 [22: 22: 24: 24] sts from back, then 5 sts up left side of back neck.
98 [102: 102: 106: 106] sts.
Cast off knitwise (on **WS**).
See information page for finishing instructions.

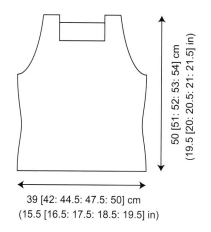

50 [51: 52: 53: 54] cm
(19.5 [20: 20.5: 21: 21.5] in)

39 [42: 44.5: 47.5: 50] cm
(15.5 [16.5: 17.5: 18.5: 19.5] in)

Deckchair

YARN

One size

RYC Cashsoft DK

A	Sweet	501	7 x 50gm
B	Cream	500	6 x 50gm
C	Crush	506	2 x 50gm

NEEDLES

1 pair 4mm (no 8) (US 6) needles

3.50mm (no 9) (US E4) crochet hook

TENSION

22 sts and 30 rows to 10 cm measured over stocking stitch using 4mm (US 6) needles.

FINISHED SIZE

Completed wrap measures 147 cm (58 in) wide and 81 cm (32 in) long (excluding fringe).

CROCHET ABBREVIATION

dc = double crochet.

WRAP

Using 4mm (US 6) needles and yarn A cast on 324 sts.

Beg with a K row, work in striped st st as folls:

Rows 1 to 8: Using yarn A.

Rows 9 to 14: Using yarn B.

Rows 15 and 16: Using yarn C.

Rows 17 to 20: Using yarn B.

Rows 21 and 22: Using yarn C.

Rows 23 to 28: Using yarn B.

These 28 rows form striped st st.

Cont straight in striped st st for a further 36 rows, ending with RS facing for next row.

Keeping stripes correct, dec 1 st at each end of next and every foll 4th row to 288 sts, then on every foll alt row until 240 sts rem.

Work 1 row, ending with RS facing for next row.

Cast off 2 sts at beg of next 42 rows, then 4 sts at beg of foll 20 rows.

Cast off rem 76 sts.

MAKING UP

Press as described on the information page.

Edging

Using 3.50mm (US E4) crochet hook and yarn A, work one row of dc evenly along entire shaped row-end and cast-off edges, beg and ending at ends of cast-on edge.

Fasten off.

Cut 38 cm lengths of yarn A and knot groups of 6 of these lengths through every 3rd st of edging to form fringe.

YARN

	XS	S	M	L	XL	
To fit bust	81	86	91	97	102	cm
	32	34	36	38	40	in

RYC Cashsoft 4 ply

| | 5 | 5 | 6 | 6 | 7 | x 50gm |

(photographed in Monet 423)

NEEDLES

1 pair 2¾mm (no 12) (US 2) needles
1 pair 3¼mm (no 10) (US 3) needles
2¾mm (no 12) (US 2) circular needle
Two double-pointed 2¾mm (no 12) (US 2) needles

TENSION

28 sts and 36 rows to 10 cm measured over stocking stitch using 3¼mm (US 3) needles.

BACK

Using 2¾mm (US 2) needles cast on 112 [118: 126: 132: 140] sts.
Work in g st for 4 rows, ending with RS facing for next row.
Change to 3¼mm (US 3) needles.
Beg with a K row, work in st st until back meas 3.5 [4.5: 4.5: 5.5: 5.5] cm, ending with RS facing for next row.
Dec 1 st at each end of next and every foll 8th row to 104 [110: 118: 124: 132] sts, then on every foll 6th row until 98 [104: 112: 118: 126] sts rem.
Work 9 rows, ending with RS facing for next row.
Inc 1 st at each end of next and every foll 8th row to 104 [110: 118: 124: 132] sts, then on every foll 10th row until there are 112 [118: 126: 132: 140] sts.
Work 9 rows, ending with RS facing for next row. (Back should meas 36 [37: 37: 38: 38] cm.)
Shape armholes
Cast off 5 [6: 6: 7: 7] sts at beg of next 2 rows.
102 [106: 114: 118: 126] sts.
Dec 1 st at each end of next 11 [11: 13: 13: 15] rows, then on foll 2 [3: 3: 4: 4] alt rows.
76 [78: 82: 84: 88] sts.
Cont straight until armhole meas 19 [19: 20: 20: 21] cm, ending with RS facing for next row.
Shape shoulders and back neck
Cast off 6 [6: 7: 7: 7] sts at beg of next 2 rows.
64 [66: 68: 70: 74] sts.

Next row (RS): Cast off 6 [6: 7: 7: 7] sts, K until there are 10 [10: 10: 10: 12] sts on right needle and turn, leaving rem sts on a holder.
Work each side of neck separately.
Cast off 4 sts at beg of next row.
Cast off rem 6 [6: 6: 6: 8] sts.
With RS facing, rejoin yarn to rem sts, cast off centre 32 [34: 34: 36: 36] sts, K to end.
Complete to match first side, reversing shapings.

LEFT FRONT

Using 2¾mm (US 2) needles cast on 93 [96: 100: 103: 107] sts.
Work in g st for 4 rows, ending with RS facing for next row.
Change to 3 1/4mm (US 3) needles.
Beg with a K row, work in st st until left front meas 3.5 [4.5: 4.5: 5.5: 5.5] cm, ending with RS facing for next row.
Dec 1 st at beg of next and every foll 8th row to 89 [92: 96: 99: 103] sts, then on every foll 6th row until 87 [90: 94: 97: 101] sts rem.
Work 5 rows, ending with RS facing for next row.
Shape front slope
Dec 1 st at each end of next row.
85 [88: 92: 95: 99] sts.
Work 1 row.
Dec 1 st at front slope edge of next and foll 33 [36: 32: 35: 31] alt rows, then on 2 [0: 3: 1: 3] foll 3rd rows **and at same time** inc 1 st at beg (side seam edge) of 9th and 2 foll 8th rows, then on 4 foll 10th rows. 56 [58: 63: 65: 71] sts.
Work 1 [1: 0: 0: 2] rows, ending with RS facing for next row. (Left front should now match back to beg of armhole shaping.)
Shape armhole
Cast off 5 [6: 6: 7: 7] sts at beg and dec 0 [0: 0: 0: 1] st at end of next row. 51 [52: 57: 58: 63] sts.
Dec 1 [1: 0: 0: 0] st at front slope edge of next row. 50 [51: 57: 58: 63] sts.
Dec 1 st at armhole edge of next 11 [11: 13: 13: 15] rows, then on foll 2 [3: 3: 4: 4] alt rows **and at same time** dec 1 st at front slope edge on 3rd [3rd: next: next: 2nd] and every foll 3rd row. 32 [32: 34: 34: 36] sts.
Dec 1 st at front slope edge **only** on 3rd [next: 3rd: next: 3rd] and every foll 3rd row until 18 [18: 20: 20: 22] sts rem.

Cont straight until left front matches back to beg of shoulder shaping, ending with RS facing for next row.
Shape shoulder
Cast off 6 [6: 7: 7: 7] sts at beg of next and foll alt row.
Work 1 row.
Cast off rem 6 [6: 6: 6: 8] sts.

RIGHT FRONT

Using 2¾mm (US 2) needles cast on 93 [96: 100: 103: 107] sts.
Work in g st for 4 rows, ending with RS facing for next row.
Change to 3¼mm (US 3) needles.
Beg with a K row, work in st st until right front meas 3.5 [4.5: 4.5: 5.5: 5.5] cm, ending with RS facing for next row.
Dec 1 st at end of next and every foll 8th row to 89 [92: 96: 99: 103] sts, then on every foll 6th row until 87 [90: 94: 97: 101] sts rem.
Complete to match left front, reversing shapings.

MAKING UP

Press as described on the information page.
Join both shoulder seams using back stitch, or mattress stitch if preferred.
Front band
With RS facing and using 2¾mm (US 2) circular needle, starting and ending at cast-on edges, pick up and knit 42 [45: 45: 48: 48] sts up right front opening edge to beg of front slope shaping, 118 [118: 121: 121: 124] sts up right front slope to shoulder, 40 [42: 42: 44: 44] sts from back, 118 [118: 121: 121: 124] sts down left front slope to beg of front slope shaping, then 42 [45: 45: 48: 48] sts down left front opening edge.
360 [368: 374: 382: 388] sts.
Work in g st for 2 rows.
Cast off knitwise (on **WS**).
Armhole borders (both alike)
With RS facing and using 2¾mm (US 2) needles, pick up and knit 120 [122: 128: 130: 136] sts evenly all round armhole edge.
Work in g st for 2 rows.
Cast off knitwise (on **WS**).
See information page for finishing instructions.

Left tie

Using 2¾mm (US 2) double-pointed needles cast on 3 sts.

Row 1 (RS): K3, *without turning slip these 3 sts to opposite end of needle and bring yarn to opposite end of work pulling it quite tightly across WS of work, K these 3 sts again, rep from * until tie is 64 cm long, K3tog and fasten off.

Right tie

Work as given for left tie, repeating from * until tie is 31 cm long.

See information page for finishing instructions, leaving an opening in left side seam level with beg of front slope shaping. Attach ends of ties to front opening edges level with beg of front slope shaping.

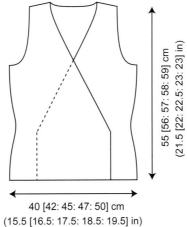

55 [56: 57: 58: 59] cm
(21.5 [22: 22.5: 23: 23] in)

40 [42: 45: 47: 50] cm
(15.5 [16.5: 17.5: 18.5: 19.5] in)

YARN
RYC Cashcotton 4 ply

13 x 50gm

(photographed in Chintz 906)

CROCHET HOOK
2.50mm (no 12) (US C2) crochet hook

TENSION
26 sts and 12 rows to 10 cm measured over pattern using 2.50mm (US C2) crochet hook.

CROCHET ABBREVIATIONS
ch = chain; **dc** = double crochet; **sp(s)** = space(s); **ss** = slip stitch; **tr** = treble; **cluster** = *yoh and insert hook into "ch sp" formed by tr just worked, yoh and draw loop through, yoh and draw through 2 loops, rep from * twice more, yoh and draw through all 4 loops on hook; **yoh** = yarn over hook.

BACK and FRONT (both alike)
Using 2.50mm (US C2) hook, make 158 ch.
Row 1 (RS): 1 tr into 6th ch from hook, *1 ch, miss 1 ch, 1 tr into next ch, rep from * to end, turn. 155 sts, 77 ch sps.
Place first blue marker at base of beg of last row, and first red marker at base of end of last row.
Cont in patt as folls:
Row 1: 4 ch (counts as 1 tr and 1 ch), miss (1 tr and 1 ch), 1 tr into next tr, *1 ch, miss 1 ch, 1 tr into next tr, rep from * to end, working tr at end of last rep into 3rd of 4 ch at beg of previous row, turn.
Rows 2 to 5: As row 1.
Row 6: 3 ch (counts as 1 tr), miss tr at end of previous row, *1 tr into next ch, 1 tr into next tr, rep from * to end, working tr at end of last rep into 3rd of 4 ch at beg of previous row, turn.
Row 7: 3 ch (counts as 1 tr), miss tr at end of previous row, 1 tr into next tr, *3 ch, 1 cluster around last tr, miss 2 tr, 1 tr into next tr, rep from * to end, working tr at end of last rep into top of 3 ch at beg of previous row, turn. 51 clusters.
Row 8: 3 ch (counts as 1 tr), 1 tr between tr at end of previous row and next cluster, *3 ch, 1 cluster around last tr, 1 tr between next 2 clusters of previous row, rep from * to end,

working tr at end of last rep into top of 3 ch at beg of previous row, turn.
Row 9: As row 8.
Row 10: 5 ch (counts as 1 tr and 2 ch), 1 tr between first 2 clusters, *2 ch, 1 tr between next 2 clusters, rep from * to end, working last tr between last cluster and 3 ch at beg of previous row, 1 tr into top of 3 ch at beg of previous row, turn.
Row 11: 3 ch (counts as 1 tr), miss tr at end of previous row, 1 tr into next tr, *2 tr into next ch sp, 1 tr into next tr, rep from * to end, working tr at end of last rep into 3rd of 5 ch at beg of previous row, turn. 155 sts.
Row 12: 4 ch (counts as 1 tr and 1 ch), miss last 2 tr of previous row, 1 tr into next tr, *1 ch, miss 1 tr, 1 tr into next tr, rep from * to end, working tr at end of last rep into top of 3 ch at beg of previous row, turn.
These 12 rows form patt.
Cont in patt until work meas 30 cm.
Place second red marker along side of work at top of last row, directly above first red marker.

Cont straight until work meas approx 90 cm, ending after patt row 5.
Fasten off.
Place second blue marker directly above red markers at one corner of top of last row.

MAKING UP
Press as described on the information page.
Join pieces together by matching first red and blue markers on one piece to second red and blue markers on other piece.
Edging
Using 2.50mm (US C2) crochet hook and with RS facing, rejoin yarn to outer edge of poncho, 1 ch (does NOT count as st), work 1 round of dc evenly around entire outer edge, ending with ss to first dc.
Fasten off.
Work edging around neck edge in same way.
Cut 40 cm lengths of yarn and knot groups of 3 of these lengths through every 3rd dc around outer edge of poncho as in photograph to form fringe.

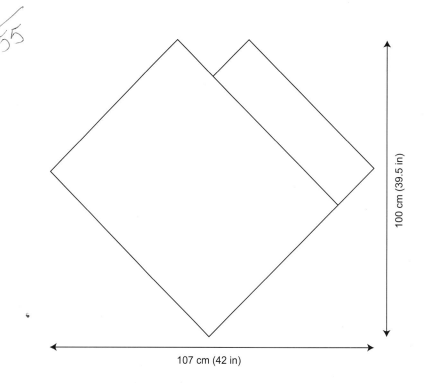

100 cm (39.5 in)

107 cm (42 in)